Words in Pictures   My Day
Mots en Images
Ma Journée

Illustrated by Elena Kisenkova

Paints
Peintures

Apple
Pomme

Alarm clock
Réveil

Pencils
Crayons

www.kidkiddos.com
Copyright ©2024 by KidKiddos Books Ltd.
support@kidkiddos.com

All rights reserved. No part of this book may be reproduced in any form or by any electronic or mechanical means, including information storage and retrieval systems, without written permission from the publisher, except in the case of a reviewer, who may quote brief passages embodied in critical articles or in a review.
First edition, 2025

Library and Archives Canada Cataloguing in Publication
Words in Pictures - My Day (English French Bilingual edition)
ISBN: 978-1-77959-359-7 paperback
ISBN: 978-1-77959-360-3 hardcover
ISBN: 978-1-77959-358-0 eBook

I wake up
Je me réveille

Curtain
Rideau

Clothes
Vêtements

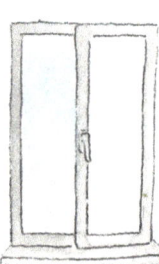

Window
Fenêtre

Carpet
Tapis

Bed
Lit

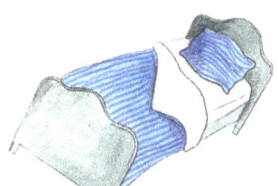

Sun
Soleil

Alarm clock
Réveil

Bird
Oiseau

Plant
Plante

Glass of water
Verre d'eau

Toothbrush
Brosse à dents

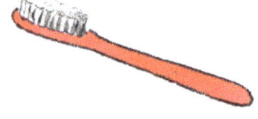

Sink
Lavabo

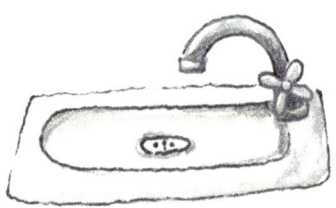

Toothpaste
Dentifrice

Towel
Serviette

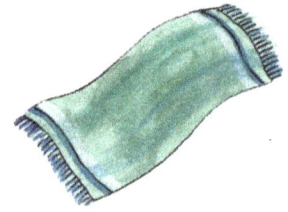

I brush my teeth

Je me brosse les dents

Mmm... Strawberry toothpaste!
Mmm... Dentifrice à la fraise!

Water
Eau

Soap
Savon

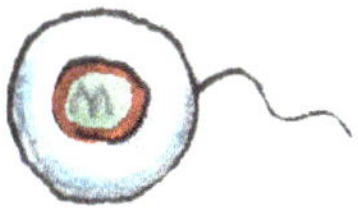

Dental floss
Fil dentaire

Drop
Goutte

I dress up
Je m'habille

What t-shirt should I wear?
Quel t-shirt devrais-je porter?

Cap
Casquette

Socks
Chaussettes

Hanger
Cintre

Pants
Pantalon

Mirror
Miroir

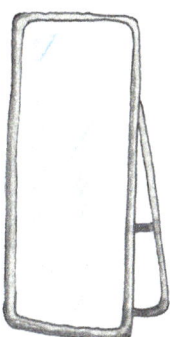

Belt
Ceinture

Shoes
Chaussures

T-shirt
T-shirt

Dresser
Commode

I eat breakfast
Je prends mon petit-déjeuner

Yogurt
Yaourt

Orange
Orange

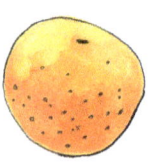

Newspaper
Journal

Banana
Banane

Milk
Lait

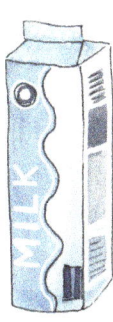

Juice
Jus

Egg
Œuf

Apple
Pomme

Bread
Pain

Sponge
Éponge

Apron
Tablier

Kettle
Bouilloire

Fork
Fourchette

Look how shiny they are!
Regardez comme ils brillent!

Spoon
Cuillère

Knife
Couteau

Dustpan
Pelle à poussière

I Help in the Kitchen
J'aide dans la cuisine

Broom
Balai

Trash can
Poubelle

Plate
Assiette

I go to school
Je vais à l'école

Fountain
Fontaine

Traffic light
Feu de circulation

Flowers
Fleurs

Watch
Montre

Duck
Canard

Car
Voiture

Bicycle
Vélo

Tree
Arbre

Squirrel
Écureuil

I meet my friends
Je retrouve mes amis

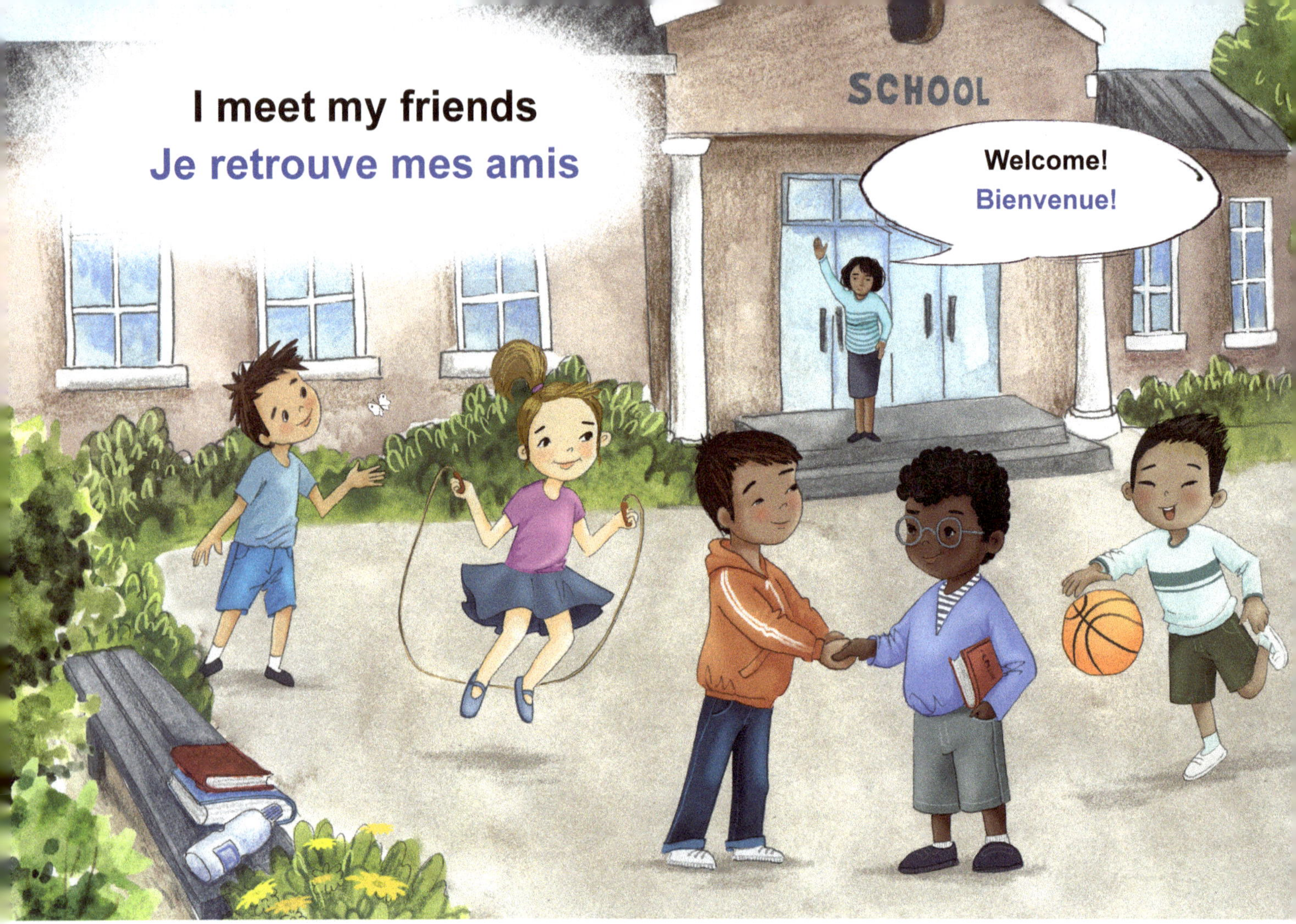
SCHOOL
Welcome!
Bienvenue!

Skipping rope
Corde à sauter

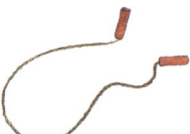

Ball
Ballon

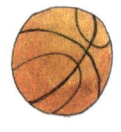

Bus
Bus

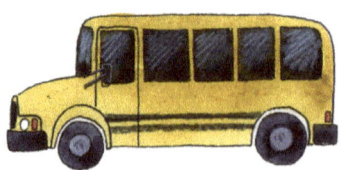

Water bottle
Bouteille d'eau

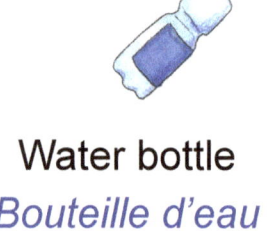

Handshake
Poignée de main

Hug
Câlin

Hello!
Bonjour !

Smile
Sourire

Backpack
Sac à dos

Notebook
Cahier

Scissors
Ciseaux

Ruler
Règle

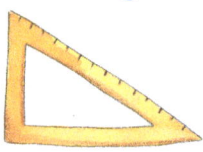

Markers
Marqueurs

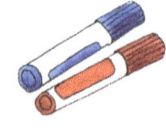

Map
Carte

I learn
J'apprends

Pencils
Crayons

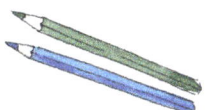

Blackboard
Tableau noir

Paints
Peintures

I go to the zoo
Je vais au zoo

Parrot
Perroquet

Monkey
Singe

Flamingo
Flamant rose

Zebra
Zèbre

Giraffe
Girafe

Lion
Lion

Map
Carte

Elephant
Éléphant

I come back home
Je rentre à la maison

Photo
Photo

Umbrella
Parapluie

Slippers
Chaussons

Vase
Vase

Sofa
Canapé

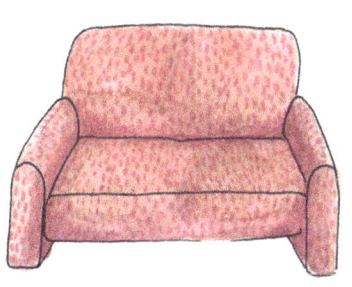

Bag
Sac

Door
Porte

Dog
Chien

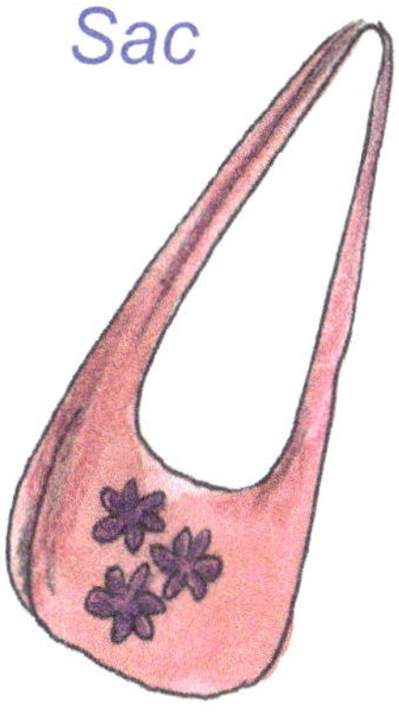

I eat dinner
Je dîne

Sausage
Saucisse

Carrots
Carottes

Salt
Sel

Napkins
Serviettes

Stove
Cuisinière

Chicken
Poulet

Salad
Salade

Cucumbers
Concombres

Tomatoes
Tomates

Cupcake
Petit gâteau

I take a bath
Je prends un bain

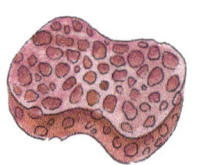

Sponge
Éponge

Shampoo
Shampoing

Duck
Canard

Boat
Bateau

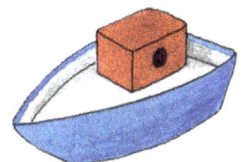

Robe
Peignoir

Towel
Serviette

Soap bubbles
Bulles de savon

Bathtub
Baignoire

Dinosaur
Dinosaure

Glasses
Lunettes

Book
Livre

I read a book
Je lis un livre

Stars
Étoiles

Cat
Chat

Moon
Lune

Slippers
Chaussons

Armchair
Fauteuil

I go to sleep
Je vais dormir

Teddy bear
Ours en peluche

Lamp
Lampe

Nightstand
Table de nuit

Drawing
Dessin

Rug
Tapis

Night sky
Ciel nocturne

Pillow
Oreiller

Blanket
Couverture

www.ingramcontent.com/pod-product-compliance
Lightning Source LLC
Chambersburg PA
CBHW042356070526
44585CB00028B/2954